Ms. V's Vacation

Read-to-Me™

The Letter People® and Read-to-Me™ are trademarks of ABRAMS & COMPANY Publishers, Inc.

Visit our Web site at www.letterpeople.com

Printed in the United States of America   ISBN: 0-7665-1222-3

          1 2 3 4 5 6 7 8 9 0   1 0 9 8 7 6 5 4 3 2

                                                                                085401V

Ms. V's Vacation

Written by Patricia W. Abrams • **Illustrated by Darcy Bell-Myers**

Ms. V loved growing vegetables. But she didn't love the crows stealing from her garden.

"That's it! I give up! I'll never plant another vegetable!" she shouted in her loudest voice as the crows gobbled up all her hard work.

"I need a vacation!" she said. "I'm going on a voyage around the world."

Ms. V's vacation began with a train trip to Virginia. She rode horses there every day.

"This is almost as much fun as planting vegetables," she thought.

"I'll miss you," Ms. V said, patting her horse's neck. "I'll keep my riding boots to remember my visit to Virginia."

Off Ms. V flew to her next stop—
Venezuela! There she danced and sang and
hiked in the tall mountains. And she tasted
some very good food.

"This *arepa* is delicious!" she said. "It's
made from corn. I'll bet I could make this
bread with corn from my garden."

But then she remembered that she'd
given up gardening for good.

"I'll miss Venezuela," she said. "I'll keep my beads and my shawl as souvenirs. They'll help me remember my visit."

Next, Ms. V flew to Africa. At Victoria Falls, she videotaped a very big rainbow.

"Wow!" she said. "The colors in the rainbow remind me of the colorful clothes in Africa. This green and orange and violet skirt will help me remember my visit."

But the bright colors also reminded her of the peppers and carrots and eggplants in her garden.

Ms. V left Africa on a big ship. She sailed for days until she reached Italy.

When she visited the city of Venice, she couldn't believe her eyes! The roadways were filled with water! People traveled in boats called gondolas.

"I love Venice! This violin will help me remember it," she said, playing a tune.

The night before she left Venice, Ms. V went out for a very special supper. Spaghetti!

"This sauce is made from the best tomatoes in the world!" she said. It made her think of the tomatoes in her own vegetable garden back home.

The next day, Ms. V flew off on the last part of her voyage. She visited a village in Vietnam. As she rode her bike, she saw villagers carrying baskets of vegetables.

"I used to grow vegetables like those," she thought. She began to miss her garden.

"I'll keep my hat to remind me of this beautiful place," she said as she packed her suitcase for her final trip—home.

When Ms. V returned home, her garden was empty. The crows had eaten all the vegetables.

"You'll never ruin my hard work again!" Ms. V called out to the crows waiting in the trees. "You won't find any more vegetables in this garden!"

Days passed. Ms. V felt sad.

"I miss my garden," she said, "and I miss my vacation."

She took out her souvenirs and put them on. She closed her eyes and thought of the places she had visited.

"I wish I could have some of that delicious *arepa* I had in Venezuela . . . or that terrific tomato sauce I had in Venice," she sighed. "I wish I could see the bright colors of the rainbow at Victoria Falls."

Suddenly, Ms. V jumped up and headed for her garden.

"I won't let those crows stop me!" she said. "I'll plant my own corn and carrots and tomatoes and peppers and eggplants. That's how I'll remember my wonderful vacation!"

19

Ms. V worked fast. She began to get very hot. One by one, she took off her souvenirs and hung them on her rake.

When she was finished planting, she stood up and looked around.

"Hey, where are all the crows?" she wondered.

The crows sat in a tree branch. They stared and stared at the garden, but they would not go near it.

"Something is scaring them away," said Ms. V. "What could they be afraid of?"

Then she turned around.

"It's a scarecrow!" Ms. V laughed. "A scarecrow made from my souvenirs!"

And from that moment on, the crows never ate Ms. V's vegetables again.

"Victory at last!" she smiled.

The Letter People Company

a division of
ABRAMS & COMPANY Publishers, Inc.
61 Mattatuck Heights
Waterbury, CT 06705
www.letterpeople.com
1–800–227–9120

🐙 Read-to-Me™

Who Will Help Ms. A?
Beautiful Buttons: A Biography of Mr. B
The Clue (Mr. C)
The Dinosaur Detective (Mr. D)
Is It an Earthquake? (Ms. E)
The Fib (Ms. F)
Where Does the Garbage Go? (Mr. G)
The Right Day for a Haircut (Mr. H)
Incredible Insects: A Poetry ANThology (Mr. I)
The Jazz Jamboree (Ms. J)
KABOOM! (Ms. K)
Ha! Ha! Ha! (Ms. L)
The More the Merrier! (Mr. M)
Not Now, Mr. N!
The Opposite Obstacle Course (Mr. O)
The Perfect Pet (Ms. P)
I'm Glad I Asked (Mr. Q)
Real Friends (Mr. R)
A Super Day for Sailing (Ms. S)
Time for a Taxi (Ms. T)
There's No Space Like Home (Ms. U)
Ms. V's Vacation
Weather Watch (Ms. W)
I'm Different (Mr. X)
Just for You (Ms. Y)
Who's New at the Zoo? (Mr. Z)
